BEYOND THE FAÇADE

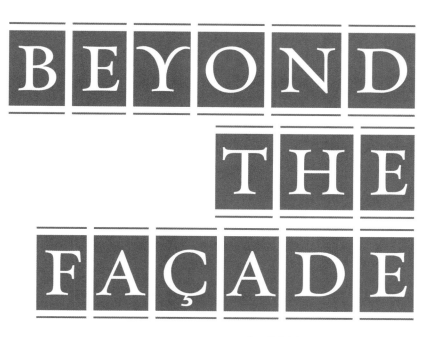

BEYOND THE FAÇADE

A SYNAGOGUE
A RESTORATION
A LEGACY

MUSEUM AT ELDRIDGE STREET

WRITTEN BY LARRY BORTNIKER
FOREWORD BY ROBERTA BRANDES GRATZ
AFTERWORD BY BONNIE DIMUN, EXECUTIVE EDITOR
EDITED BY NANCY JOHNSON

SCALA

First published in 2011 by Scala Publishers Limited
Northburgh Street
10 Northburgh House
London EC1V 0AT
United Kingdom

Distributed outside the Museum at Eldridge Street
in the booktrade by
Antique Collectors' Club Limited
6 West 18th Street, 4th floor
New York, NY 10011
United States of America

ISBN: 978-1-85759-718-9

Printed and bound in Singapore
10 9 8 7 6 5 4 3 2 1

For information write:

Museum at Eldridge Street

12 Eldridge Street

New York, NY 10002

212.219.0888

Designed by Mindy Lang
Cover photo: Whitney Cox
Half title page photo: Frank Hallam Day
Frontispiece: Amy R. Sperling

CONTENTS

ACKNOWLEDGMENTS

The dream of saving the Eldridge Street Synagogue represents a collective commitment of great magnitude which has brought us to this day. I am struck by all those who contributed to this effort, reaching back to the community of Jews who came to America for a new life in the 19th century, to those who toiled to preserve and honor their legacy in the 20th and now in the 21st centuries, bringing a beautiful house of worship back to life. This book is a record of that monumental task, and of the beauty, spirit, and community that has been preserved. The many people associated with *Beyond the Façade* have contributed to documenting, in the most beautiful way, the saving of this site and the legacy it represents.

First and foremost, the Board of Trustees, chaired by Michael Weinstein, was and continues to be the guiding force behind the restoration of the synagogue and the creation of the Museum at Eldridge Street. With the financial support of the Board and the thousands who contributed to this grass roots effort, there was absolute resolve to complete this endeavor. We could not have been more fortunate in finding those who truly cared about preserving the memory of those who struggled for us by coming to this country and the embodiment of their legacy in the Eldridge Street Synagogue.

I have always believed that ours is a story best told in pictures. We are grateful to the many photographers whose work fills these pages. They saw the beauty of the building, even at its most dilapidated, capturing the restoration in process and documenting the latest additions.

Larry Bortniker was the perfect writer to bring these pictures and the story they document vividly to life. Mindy Lang, long associated with the Eldridge Street Project, expertly united words and pictures to create a beautifully designed volume. Nancy Johnson, a gem of an editor under our own roof, brought the pieces together with care and creativity; her special attention to detail was exactly what this project needed.

I must take the opportunity to hail the entire Museum staff now and over the years. Their contributions are tangible in this building. I especially want to thank Amy Stein Milford, Eva Bruné, and Hanna Griff-Sleven who all offered invaluable assistance in the creation of this book. Amy's work in developing a new architectural tour was a tremendous simultaneous effort, complementing this book and underscoring our commitment to the Eldridge Street restoration story.

Roberta Brandes Gratz, author and journalist, contributed her singular perspective as founder of the Eldridge Street Project and its first Executive Director. She was among the first to comprehend the importance of the Eldridge Street Synagogue and worked tirelessly to preserve it.

I am and will continue to be grateful to our docents who greeted and educated our visitors through the days of truly deplorable conditions, yet today, through their love of this project, remain our most valuable asset, telling the story *Beyond the Façade*.

Forever grateful...
Bonnie Dimun
Executive Director, Museum at Eldridge Street

Publication of *Beyond the Façade* was made possible by the generous contributions of the following:

Arlene and Morris Goldfarb
Daniel and Joanna S. Rose
Sheila and Joseph B. Rosenblatt
Rhonda and Robert Silver
Michael Weinstein
Brad Wiley
Judy Francis Zankel
The Dimun Family

FOREWORD
FLASHLIGHT INTO HISTORY

ROBERTA BRANDES GRATZ

December, 1982.
The Eldridge Street Synagogue.

Pigeons roosted in the attic and flew in and out of missing windows. Dust was so thick on the pews that you could carve your initials in it. Water was pouring through one corner of the roof. Prayer books were left strewn about. Little objects that worshippers long ago had left behind, including crystal drinking glasses, were randomly scattered. Pieces of stained glass from broken windows were everywhere.

When I first walked in, I took one look and said: If we don't save this building, we would have to reinvent it someday. The full story of Jews in America can't be told without this building.

Decades before, congregants had worshipped one day and closed the upstairs sanctuary the next, moving downstairs to the *bes medrash* where a small congregation still worships today. Through the dust, despite the pigeons, and beyond the many broken elements, a haunting beauty came through. Sunlight streaming through the windows shone on the floating particles of dust like a flashlight into history. But it wasn't just the beauty that was so striking. That can be found in many historic houses of worship. Nor was the survival of so many decorative elements, original and irreplaceable, which had never been subjected to unfortunate modernization. The ghosts of history were here. Even if my own great grandparents had not worshipped here, I could still feel their presence among the East European Jews who had created this building.

Sure, Touro, Charleston, Baltimore all have beautifully preserved and historically significant synagogues. In New York City as well, Shearith Israel, Temple Emmanu-El, and Central Synagogue are steeped in chapters of our history that reflect the Jews' complicated weaving into the fabric of American society. But those houses of worship represent the Sephardic and German waves of immigration, a very different tale than the worshippers at Eldridge. This was the gateway to America for traditionally observant East Europeans, the first building they built as a synagogue. Representing the forebears of about three-quarters of all the Jews living in the United States, these immigrants from the Russian and Austrian empires were the largest wave of Jewish immigration.

It wasn't until 1986 that the Eldridge Street Project was organized and the long road to restoration began. The long list of dedicated Board members, generous donors, and innovative staff was just beginning to assemble but each of those many critical participants recognized what needed to be done. All shared in moving it along, all understood the unique place in history that is held by this synagogue.

For the Lower East Side, the Eldridge Synagogue had been a major center of Jewish life, *the* synagogue among many. For so many new arrivals, their story started here. For some, we learned from former congregants, it was an occasional visit. For others, membership here was the pride of their family.

For hundreds of years, East European Jews worshipped in unprepossessing spaces, vernacular in style, meant to blend in with local buildings so as not to attract undo attention. Most East European Jews had fled pogroms and other life threats to settle here. At first, they only worshipped here in small local synagogues, called *shteibeles*. But when they realized they were finally in a place where they could worship openly and freely, they built the Eldridge Street Synagogue.

Just as an artifact of architectural history, Eldridge stands out. It is grand, embellished, and elegant. Boldly it proclaims its Jewishness. Stars of David are everywhere, a clear statement of "we are here, we are Jewish, we are free." No longer was it necessary to hide their religious affiliation; instead, America provided the opportunity to celebrate it. Eldridge is that celebration in stone.

By my first visit in 1982, deterioration threatened the synagogue's survival. The most dramatic result of neglect was visible down in the four-foot-high dirt-floor crawl space. The dirt under one of the foundation walls had been washed away, caused by a small leak of probably 50 years. The 75-bulb sanctuary chandelier had no business still hanging. Engineers told us it should have fallen down years ago. Even the roof was highly compromised, though the water pouring in was still confined to one corner. When the roof starts to go, rescue is most difficult. At that point I sensed that this building was being held up by a string from heaven.

Despite the dire conditions, some things miraculously survived intact. The handcarved mahogany ark with its red velvet lining could still be opened with one finger in the sliding door. Many of the spatterware spitoons that sat at the end of each pew were still in place. Piles of dishes and big *cholent* pots were found in a closet. All the stained glass remained within its original window or on the floor where it had fallen. From top to bottom, this was an intact treasure. And what was not in place or couldn't be figured out was mostly explained in the minutes of the congregation dating from before construction in 1886 through the 1950s.

There were moments, too, when the building revealed traces of the history that had unfolded within its walls. When the pews were removed for the work to begin, I could see deep depressions in the floor. I was stunned by what they represented. I could imagine, I could hear, thousands of feet shuffling between the pews, imparting a small sense of how well used this synagogue had been.

And then there was the day I was sitting in the balcony. I thought of the hard lives so many of the worshippers led, working in overcrowded sweatshops, living in crowded quarters, walking the teeming streets. What a refuge this must have been, the one place worshippers could feel valued. After all, if one is worthy to pray in such a magnificent place, that meant something.

As I sat there and felt the rich texture of social history revealed here, I was acutely aware the overarching responsibility we have to protect these precious vessels of yesterday's stories.

Why Save a Synagogue?

I was often challenged by people unaware of the touchstones of Jewish history remaining on the Lower East Side, especially this one. "Why do you want to save an old synagogue in Chinatown?" they asked. We had so many different answers, each one valid. We created a tour, "From Ellis to Eldridge," when tourist interest was just emerging. Ellis Island had just reopened, newly restored. Suddenly, interest in immigrant history was on the public mind. And the Lower East Side was where an immigrant's story began after the Ellis Island ferry landed. The Lower East Side Tenement Museum and the Museum of Chinese in America also evolved to capture different chapters of the immigrant story.

Here was the ultimate urban neighborhood, the cradle of immigration, the gateway for millions of new Americans. Here was an urban fabric very much the same as it was 100 years earlier. Red brick tenements, now home to mostly Chinese, were once home to Germans, Russians, and Italians, Protestants, Catholics, and Jews. Storefronts with similar businesses to 100 years ago— discount fashions, household goods, specialty foods—were owned by new entrepreneurs. They would move on, inevitably, as their predecessors had done. The new arrivals were absorbed, given a chance to adjust, find work, start a business, educate themselves and their children.

The buildings, declared a "slum" decades earlier, looked the same, but they were fully occupied with residents and entrepreneurial activity. Change—positive, creative, enduring change—had swept over this area of the Lower East Side but the buildings hadn't been torn down to make it happen. In fact, the physical fabric of this neighborhood—with its variety of building types—was conducive to that process of change and growth, fertile ground for adaptation, innovation and growth.

I watched storefronts become Buddhist Temples the way they had become synagogues a century earlier. The Garden Cafeteria became a Chinese restaurant. The Canal Street Dairy, our favorite kosher eating place, had a Yiddish-speaking-only cook who made the best blintzes ever tasted. It closed to become an electronics store. One by one the Jewish merchants sold to the new arrivals. Grand Street was still 100 percent Jewish-owned dry goods and assorted retail shops when I first visited the synagogue; it became an Asian food market with shoppers flooding in from all over the city. Chinatown was still a few blocks to the west when we began. The Bowery was the boundary. Chinatown has since come several blocks east from its traditional boundaries. It happened over the course of more than a decade. Urban change unfolded daily before my eyes on the surrounding streets.

Stand in front of the synagogue, as I like to tell visitors to do. Look up and down the block and look at the store signs. Just blink and in your mind's eye convert those Chinese characters on the signs to Hebrew and Yiddish. At that moment, you can see how the fundamental absorption process has continued unabated. The people, the language, and the signs have changed but the process, the fundamental urbanism, remains strong. In other areas of the Lower East Side, the transformation has been equally dramatic. Today, in fact, increasingly upscale streets like Orchard and Ludlow, with popular boutiques, restaurants, and high-priced condos, are hard to recognize for what they once were.

Neighborhood change is not the only kind of change observed over the course of this 25-year effort. Remember, in the mid-80s, the city was still emerging out of its lowest point of the 1970s. Past images and feelings die hard. No one viewed the Lower East Side then as a hip place. In fact, many uptowners wouldn't venture anywhere near it.

It was challenging in the mid-80s to lure a few people to join the board of the Eldridge Street Project. It was also almost impossible to get people to come down to see it. So, we did the next best thing. Film maker Leonard Majzlin and historian Richard Rabinowitz created a short video that we took to living rooms uptown where interested hosts invited friends to come hear about the restoration effort. Fundraising in this way proceeded ever so slowly and in very small increments. But at least it moved forward.

Discouragement Not Allowed

There was no time to be discouraged. Restoring a landmark that has been abandoned by those most connected to it historically is only for the young, the persistent, and the deeply committed, and surely not for the faint of heart. Potential donors were extremely skeptical. Even those who valued the idea of preservation doubted we could pull it off. We kept reinventing arguments for the effort, repeatedly having to explain why it was worth doing, important, valuable, urgent.

People we thought would find this appealing were often more than not interested; they were almost repelled by the idea. "I spent my whole life leaving the Lower East Side," one told me, "and now you want me to come back?"

Our three earliest generous supporters gave us much needed credentials as well as critical financial aid before the actual Eldridge Street Project was launched in 1986. Joy Ungerleider Mayerson gave us credibility in the Jewish fundraising world; Joan K. Davidson and Brooke Astor in the preservation and foundation worlds. Mrs. Astor was the doyenne of New York City philanthropy. She considered this an important project. In fact, she talked about it at dinner parties around town, telling many people that you could open the ark with one finger. That endorsement meant everything.

Actually, the slow road to success worked in our favor. We had time to do serious historical research about both the building and the people who used it. If we had had all the money early, we might have ruined the building, replaced things that could have been salvaged, refinished others that could have been conserved and in many ways, erased the patina of time. In the mid-1980s the world of historic preservation, restoration, and conservation was not nearly at its current level of sophistication and nuance. The idea of preserving the "layers" of history reflected in the architecture was not yet widely accepted. A long time away was recognition of historic preservation as the building block for truly sustainable, "green" architecture. Even today, this understanding is just emerging.

Fundraising was slow. Skepticism was hard to fight. We determined, however, that it was important to demonstrate the variety of educational, artistic, and entertainment uses that were possible here, beyond the ongoing religious purpose. Amy Waterman, who worked on some of the original research while at the American History Workshop, came on as director while I stayed on the Board. A small, brilliant staff was assembled. They created endless innovative programming: musicales, art exhibits, lectures, varied educational programs for public school children, *mitzvah* clean-up days for *bar* and *bat mitzvah* classes, holiday celebrations. Bonnie Dimun succeeded Amy, oversaw the completion of the restoration, and dramatically expanded the variety of that interpretive programming into a full-fledged museum. New programs, never done anywhere else, continue to be developed.

Nothing like the restoration of Eldridge had really been done. We had few models to learn from. Eldridge was so intact, even if degraded, that the challenge was to retain all that was left while inserting modern systems for heavy contemporary use. Many other landmarks, upgraded over time, had lost so much original fabric and had been so heavily compromised that new adjustments were easier to make than on a building so pure.

Time allowed us to learn the building, understand its religious and social history. Early on, we had a lot of wrong information. The image of the poor, starving refugee had to be modified to include the immigrants who came with resources. We first thought the congregation was composed mostly of recent arrivals. Later we learned that Eldridge emerged out of earlier congregations at other locations, attracting immigrants from Central and not just East European Jewry. The minutes of the congregation, written in a somewhat crude Yiddish and difficult to translate, told us that some congregants paid $1,000 for a High Holiday seat in the 1880s. That was big money then. In fact, one of the aspects that makes Eldridge unique as a synagogue restoration project is the existence of those minutes that tell the story of the people and the building. Encapsuled in this complete package is such a gold mine of religious and social history.

In the end, the preservation of this edifice was in fact staunching the loss of memory, a "mission of memory," Bill Moyers called it. In the era of immigrant assimilation into American society when so many Jews moved uptown or out of town, many connections were lost to all things Jewish—historical and cultural. The future was what was important; the past for many—often a painful past—was to be put behind. This, of course, parallels the story of many ethnic and religious groups across American history. Even today, with the remarkable embracing of city life by people of all backgrounds, the Lower East Side is both home and a playground for the young with little or no knowledge of the area's history.

So the rescue, preservation/conservation, and new use of Eldridge as both an ongoing synagogue and new museum has multiple layers of profound importance. Its significance as an architectural treasure is clearly visible but its rescue as a treasured vessel of deep memory is yet to be fully absorbed.

Its significance as a way of honoring our forebears is also understood but its testimony to our changing view of urban life and New York history is yet to be appreciated. Our understanding of this building has changed over time and will continue to change; the public understanding of the value of the built environment is still in its infancy, or perhaps adolescence.

Layers of city buildings, the infinite variety built over time, reflect layers of human activity and history. We no longer can destroy and replace at will. A city is composed of so many kinds of actions reflecting millions of decisions of ordinary people not controlled by a singular voice. Many of those voices echo from the stones and stars of Eldridge as they do in the bricks and stairwells of buildings all around the synagogue.

In my mind's eye, I always knew Eldridge would one day look the way it does in all its current glory. I lived with that future image so long that it became part of my DNA. I didn't expect to live long enough, however, to either ride the handicap elevator or wrestle with the dilemma of what to do about the lost rose window—to recreate what we didn't really know existed originally or to insert a 21st-century contribution to this incomparable landmark. I never dreamed such a perfect solution could be created as has been done by Kiki Smith and Deborah Gans.

December, 1982.

If I knew then what I know now, I never would have had the audacity to assume this restoration and museum creation could be done. But I was ignorant, stubborn, and inspired, and fortunately for this synagogue and the memories it will keep alive, hundreds of equally inspired people joined the effort, advocated on its behalf, funded its restoration, and signed on to keep the building and the stories alive for at least the next 100 years. Fortunately, as well, a new generation is signing on in big ways and small to keep the building and the stories alive. This generation has ties to the New York of today and is even farther removed from the legendary history of both the area and the synagogue. It really does take a village and I am forever grateful to my fellow Board members and wonderful staff for sharing the audacity to believe that it should—and could—be done.

Irving R. Wiles, *Reading from the Scroll at the Eldridge Street Synagogue,* an illustration
for "The Jews in New York," by Richard Wheatley. Century Magazine, January 1892

INTRODUCTION

s *The World of Our Fathers* becomes the world of our forebears, and that world disappears forever, the Eldridge Street Synagogue proudly stands today as it did in its glorious heyday over a century ago—now, as always, a house of worship, but even more poignantly, one of the last remaining original Jewish signposts in the shifting cultural sands of the Lower East Side.

That it stands at all is a stirring testament to several deeply Jewish cultural traits: the need to remember, the impulse to celebrate, and the wish to instruct.

The Eldridge Street Synagogue, for this and future generations, is a lustrous repository containing 67 original gorgeous stained-glass windows, a magnificent hand-carved ark on the eastern wall, the warmest of woodwork everywhere you turn, a spectacular ceiling with a touchingly beautiful chandelier, a handsome and imposing *bimah*, doorknobs, finials, sconces—all of them painstakingly retrieved and fully restored from the ravages of time and neglect. It is composed, as well, of heart and soul and faith, of exuberance and optimism, of life in all its cycles. It is a showpiece that reminds us where we came from, what we survived, and what we can be grateful for, not only as Jews, but as Americans. It teaches us the great lesson of the timeless present—in America, anything is possible.

Indeed, the Eldridge Street Synagogue is that rarity among Jewish landmarks—one which chronicles religious freedom rather than persecution, advancement rather than destruction, joy rather than horror, one whose demise would have been attributed to upward mobility rather than to a pogrom. Would have been. But the demise of the Eldridge Street Synagogue is no longer an imminent possibility, thanks to the great efforts of the Eldridge Street Project, to the architects, artists, artisans, electricians, and plumbers who have given this magnificent monument a second life, and to the patrons and visitors who will keep it alive.

The pictures in this book tell a *Titanic*-like story— a great vessel mortally pierced by the icebergs of immigration quotas, social migration and ultimately, lack of funds, sinking helplessly in an ocean of debilitating disrepair, with only slightly more than a *minyan* of congregants left to keep it above water. This time, however, the ship has come back from the deep, as evidenced in the remarkable images you are about to see.

A once badly compromised foundation proudly supports anew an edifice of singular beauty, with every structural damage now a memory. Windows that were boarded up or covered over with plastic garbage bags are once again filled with the stained-glass panels of old. The galaxy of chips and cracks and celestial potholes that spread across the ceiling is once again a firmament of vibrant stars. And what could not be accurately recreated has been movingly reinvented, like the breathtaking new east window designed by Kiki Smith and Deborah Gans, which links the past to the future and art to architecture in one dazzling stroke.

But more than a before and after, this book is a record of what has always been. It is a record of an immigrant people, like so many other immigrant peoples, who came to these shores, for better or for worse, in search of refuge and freedom. In fact, they did a whole lot better. And so, the Eldridge Street Synagogue is a perpetual valentine in the ongoing love affair between Jewish-Americans and the City of New York.

A BRIEF HISTORY

T he period in which the Eldridge Street Synagogue emerged and thrived begins with the onset of large-scale pogroms in south-western Imperial Russia in 1881 and ends with the passing of the Immigration Act of 1924 and the National Origins Quota, also in 1924, by the US Congress. During this remarkably dynamic period of immigration, two and a half million Yiddish-speaking Ashkenazi Jews fled the Pale of Settlement (modern Poland, Lithuania, Belarus, Ukraine, and Moldova) and the Russian-controlled portions of Poland, and came to America.

More than a million and a half of them would settle on the Lower East Side.

Previous page: Unknown artist, *Kahal Adath Jeshurun, 12–16 Eldridge Street*, 1886. Watercolor mounted on cloth. Museum of the City of New York, The J. Clarence Davies Collection, 29.100.2917

New York—Welcome to the Land of Freedom—An Ocean Steamer Passing the Statue of Liberty: Scene on the Steerage Deck. Drawn by a staff artist for *Frank Leslie's Illustrated Newspaper,* July 2, 1887. Library of Congress

From early on, scores of competing congregations formed, street by street, each vying for expanded membership and solvency. In 1886, two of the more prominent ones merged—*Beth Hamedrash* ("House of Study"), a well-established congregation at 78 Allen Street which started up in the mid-1850s after a smaller wave of Russian Jewish immigration, and the newer *Holkhe Yosher Vizaner* ("Those Who Walk in Righteousness"). They renamed themselves *Kahal Adath Jeshurun* ("People's Congregation of the Just").

Its impassioned lay leaders were four successful and devout businessmen: Sender Jarmulowsky, a yeshiva scholar and millionaire banker; Isaac Gellis, a sausage maker; David Cohen, a real estate investor; and Nathan Hutkoff, a plate-glass dealer. Each would serve as president of the congregation. Through their fervent piety and keen business acumen, Kahal Adath Jeshurun quickly blossomed. It acquired lots 12, 14, and 16 on the east side of Eldridge Street, and in little more than a year, the Lower East Side's first Orthodox synagogue built from the ground up opened its doors. The event made a splash in all the newspapers, and visitors and dignitaries thronged the dedication ceremony.

Its architects, brothers Peter and Francis Herter, were two German-born Catholics who had recently arrived in America themselves. They won the commission, only their fifth in New York, on the basis of several tenements with elaborate façades and finer amenities that they designed in Yorkville and the Lower East Side. The Eldridge Street Synagogue launched their careers, bringing them subsequent commissions from Gellis, Jarmulowsky, congregants, and others in the neighborhood. They eventually designed over sixty buildings in lower Manhattan, but this would be their only synagogue.

For the next forty years, as congregants prospered and moved away, new immigrants would dependably fill their places in the pews. The Eldridge Street Synagogue continued as the preeminent mainstay of Orthodox Jewish life in the area, offering daily prayer services, study groups, a hall for celebrations, a *chevra kadisha* (burial society), and a meeting place for community concerns and conflicts, with a *mikvah* (purifying bath) conveniently located around the block. The stringent immigration laws of 1924 would end it all.

Left to right: Sender Jarmulowsky, a Talmudic scholar and bank founder, was the first president of the Eldridge Street congregation; Rabbi Avrohom Aharon Yudelovitch served as Eldridge Street rabbi from 1918–30; Rabbi Yisroel "Idel" Idelson served as Eldridge Street rabbi from 1930–43.

This ark, now in the *bes medrash* at the Eldridge Street Synagogue, was moved from the congregation's former home at 78 Allen Street for the sum of $3. Photo: © Kate Milford

Faced with the Great Depression and a decreasing membership base, the synagogue slowly declined through the1930s and 40s. Nonetheless, the congregation managed to pay off its mortgage in 1944. By the 1950s, no longer able to cover operating costs or to pay for repairs, the congregation closed the main sanctuary and worshipped in the modest *bes medrash*.

Dilapidation followed on the heels of decline. By 1970, the main sanctuary had become waterlogged, grime-covered, and increasingly more exposed to the elements. Wood had rotted; plaster had crumbled and cracked; windows had deteriorated. The pigeons roosting in the rafters greatly outnumbered the few remaining congregants, and the future of the Eldridge Street Synagogue seemed bleak, indeed.

Its unexpected return to life began in 1971, when Gerard Wolfe, a New York University professor and architectural historian, convinced the sexton to let him in to see the sanctuary. A few yanks of a crowbar and the crypt was unsealed.

The 1970s brought some attention and recognition to the synagogue.

Wolfe conducted walking tours and spearheaded a group which secured a listing on the National Register of Historic Places and a landmark designation from the New York City Landmarks Preservation Committee. Architecture writer Paul Goldberger wrote an article about the synagogue in *The New York Times,* and both he and Wolfe published books which referenced the synagogue with photographs and encomiums.

The 1980s brought organization and seed money. Attorney William Josephson discovered the synagogue on one of the walking tours conducted by Professor Wolfe. He, in turn, brought award-winning journalist and preservationist Roberta Brandes Gratz to Eldridge Street. Their involvement in the rescue efforts led to the formation of the Eldridge Street Project and resulted in substantial contributions and grants. When the Project incorporated in 1986 as a not-for-profit, nonsectarian cultural organization aimed at restoring the synagogue and creating a Jewish heritage center, Ms. Gratz assumed the directorship.

Peeling paint and layers of dust were found throughout the sanctuary, which had been sealed off for decades. Photo: Ozier Muhammed, *Newsday*

An elaborate brass chandelier still hung at the center of the sanctuary, which had been closed for decades.
Previous page: A large section of fallen plaster reveals the lath and supports for a small dome in a side bay
of the sanctuary. Photos: © Kate Milford

Plaster capitals on columns in the women's balcony were wrapped in plastic to protect them as restoration work proceeded. Photo: © Kate Milford

For the next two decades, the
synagogue would go through a
protracted period of stop-and-
start, piecemeal restoration, owing
to the difficulty of raising funds.
In 1996, it was designated a
National Historic Landmark by
the US Department of the Interior
and the National Parks Service,
and in October 2010, the restoration
was finally completed, at a total
cost of $19 million.

The Eldridge Street Project,
now renamed the Museum at
Eldridge Street, has safely delivered
this precious landmark into the
twenty-first century, and with
hope, beyond.

THE FAÇADE

pproaching the Eldridge Street Synagogue from either end of Eldridge, one can barely see it beyond the row of tenements and storefronts whose Yiddish signs were long ago re-stenciled in Chinese. Then suddenly, it appears—big, bold, a vestigial wonder: 53 feet wide, 79 feet deep, 70 feet up to the apex of its central bay—daring dimensions for a building set on a narrow side street only 20 feet wide. On the day its doors opened in September 1887, the synagogue towered over the neighborhood tenements, a structure clearly intended to impress. Its total cost—$91,907.61, including the purchase of the land—was impressive as well.

The façade is cream-colored pressed brick in running bond with molded-brick, terra cotta, and stone details. It is divided vertically into three bays, with a wider central bay flanked by narrower side towers, and horizontally into three levels that are separated by elaborate stringcourses or cornices of stone and terra cotta. Its elements are eclectic and freely combined. Since the Talmud outlines very few specifications for synagogue architecture, architects could borrow as they pleased. The gables and central rose window are Gothic; the bulk of the masonry, the heavy terra cotta surrounds, and the paired side towers are Romanesque. But, as in the interior, Moorish influences predominate, from the dramatic array of keyhole-shaped windows and doorways with their exotic horseshoe arches, to the horseshoe-arcaded parapet delineating the gable of the central bay, to the rooftop finials, to the intricate foliage patterns and geometric shapes carved into the terra cotta.

By the time the Eldridge Street Synagogue came to be, Moorish Revival had already become something of a standard for synagogue architecture, both in Europe and in America. For one thing, the style recalled the "Golden Age" in Spain, a period roughly between the tenth and twelfth centuries, when Christians, Muslims, and Jews lived in

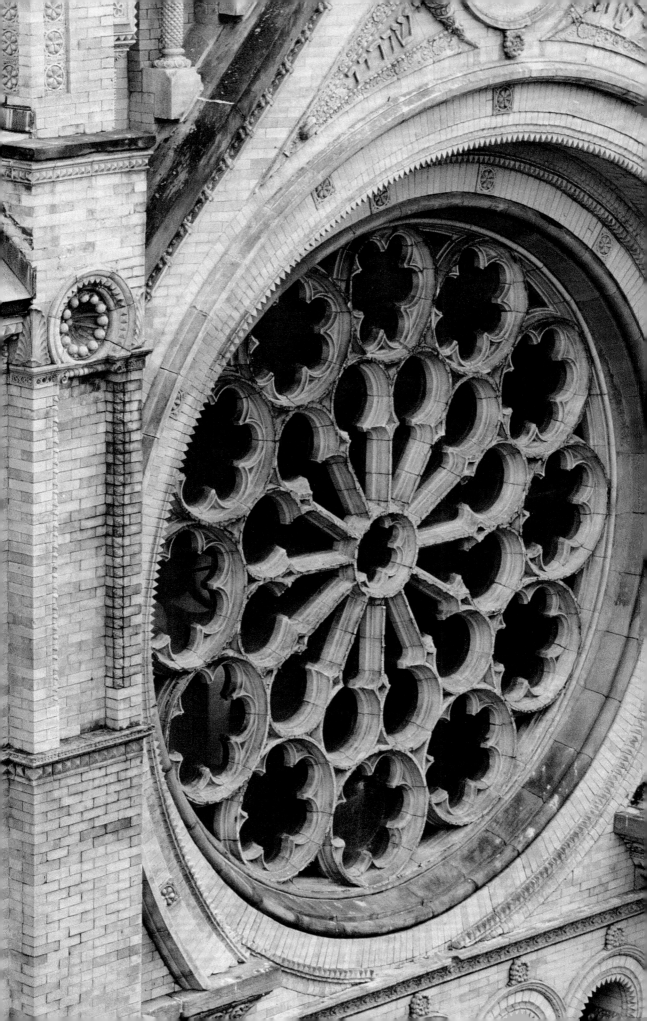

Previous page: An aerial view of the north corner of the façade shows missing stained glass in the rose and keyhole windows. Photo: Mario Morgado

The many decorative features on the façade include Moorish arches and keyhole windows; reconstructed finials along the roofline; and the congregation name, *Kahal Adath Jeshurun*, inscribed in Hebrew above the rose window. Photos: Lee Snider

ecumenical harmony and prosperity. Certainly, an apt historical metaphor for Jews in America. Beyond this, the Moorish style was completely free of Christian symbolism and associations. And so the architects of the Eldridge Street Synagogue and the leaders of the congregation Kahal Adath Jeshurun looked eastward for inspiration.

They probably also looked uptown and found some of their inspiration in the first Temple Emanu-El (1868) on Fifth Avenue and 43rd Street, a grand example of the Moorish Revival style which the smaller Eldridge Street Synagogue resembles both in proportion and design. Some historians believe the downtown congregation was in architectural competition with the Temple, which, at the time, was the cornerstone of the Reform movement in New York. What Temple Emanu-El was for Reform German Jews, the Eldridge Synagogue would be for the Orthodox Eastern European Jews of the Lower East Side.

If the synagogue's influences are various, the principal motif is singularly Jewish. Stars of David abound. They are carved into the heavy wooden doors and set in terra cotta bands. They appear atop the seven 15-foot columned finials along the roofline and in the stained glass of the Gothic rose window, thus distinguishing it from the traditional rose windows of Catholic churches. What is more, the façade groups its elements in numbers which some believe suggest a more-than-likely Old Testament significance. The three bays of the building and the three points of the central pediment represent the three patriarchs of Israel: Abraham, Isaac, and Jacob. The four doors recall the four matriarchs: Sarah, Rebecca, Leah, and Rachel. Groups of five, such as the cluster of windows at the second level, serve as reminders of the Five Books of Moses. The twelve roundels around the circumference of the Gothic rose window evoke the twelve tribes of Israel.

Unmistakably, here was a grand Jewish house of worship, the first for a community which had previously conducted its prayers in tenements, storefronts, and converted churches. The doors open, and the outer grandeur leads you to the opulence within.

Steven J. Selenfriend

Among the building's many terra cotta details are inlaid tiles with varied floral motifs and richly decorated columns. Photos: Diane Kaese

Opposite: A pigeon sits on a tower that will eventually hold a restored finial. Photo: Mario Morgado

MAIN
SANCTUARY

he spiritual center of the Eldridge Street Synagogue is the main sanctuary, which occupies most of the building's space.

Coming in from the street for the first time, the modern visitor is unprepared for the beauty and extravagance a few short steps beyond the foyer. One can only imagine what those long-ago congregants must have felt—say, the ones who had just arrived on a boat and moved into a relative's already overcrowded apartment with the hope that they would stand on their own one day soon—what must they have felt when they entered this lavish sanctuary for their first Sabbath services in America? What must they have thought as they washed their hands in the foyer before entering the synagogue—actual running water! History cannot accurately record such emotions, nor can it bring back to life the soulful melismas of the cantor, the *mazel tovs* called out at a wedding or *bar mitzvah,* or the crying of mourners during a *yizkor* memorial service.

But they resound within these walls.

The sanctuary is 3,060 square feet and follows a basic basilican plan. A balcony extends over the paired side aisles and west end and is supported by two rows of structural columns on the main level that divide the space into three longitudinal sections. In accordance with the Orthodox Jewish precept of separate seating, the women and girls would take the side tower stairs to their place in the balcony; the men and boys entered the center doors and sat below. The balcony arcade is defined by a second tier of columns that support Moorish arches—as with the façade, Moorish arches and details are everywhere, from the walls to the windows to the ark to the pews.

Looking up to the women's balcony.
Opposite: The restored women's balcony. Glass blocks that once filled the east window, visible at the left, have been replaced by a new stained-glass window. Photos: Whitney Cox

This page and opposite: The many painted surfaces in the upper level of the sanctuary include scroll designs in the spandrels, a *faux* marble finish on columns, a braided motif on arches, and stars on a blue ground in the domes. Photos: Whitney Cox

JUDITH & STANLEY ZABAR
IN HONOR OF
LORI ZABAR & MARK MARISCAL

Above the central section, 50 feet high, is a dramatic barrel-vaulted ceiling with soaring coffered vaults and a prominent dome. The effect of the ceiling is repeated in each balcony bay, where a smaller dome is supported by spherical pendentives. The many arches between and in front of the bays suggest a compressed Alhambra. Spacious yet intimate, dense yet airy, the sanctuary comfortably seats 750. It must have felt particularly dense and intimate on the High Holidays, when over 1,000 worshippers crowded its pews.

Previous page: The restoration was funded in numerous ways, including donations for honorary plaques placed on sanctuary pews.

Photo: © Peter Aaron/Esto

Above the women's balcony, smaller star-lined domes, some embellished with stained-glass oculi, echo the sanctuary's large central dome. Photo: © Peter Aaron/Esto

During prayer, Jews are required to face eastward toward Jerusalem, in the direction of King Solomon's Temple. And so, the sanctuary's focal point, the Torah ark, is at the eastern wall. Built into a small extension of the building, it is, architecturally, a holy entity unto itself. The elaborately carved walnut wood ark cleverly replicates the shape and elements of the façade. Intricate carvings, however, take the place of the façade's terra cotta ornamentation, and azure tablets inscribed with the Ten Commandments replace the rose window. The wooden finials and Stars of David on top complete the replication.

Bare light bulbs ring the tablets as they did in 1907, when the synagogue was first wired for electricity. It was hoped that the novelty would boost membership. A more sanctified glow emanates from the golden eternal light, or *Ner Tamid,* which hangs from above, symbolic of G-d's eternal and immanent presence.

The Torah ark on the synagogue's eastern wall. Photo: © Peter Aaron/Esto

Inside the ark, a three-tiered platform accommodates as many as 24 Torah scrolls. Miraculously, the original crimson velvet lining from 1887 is in pristine condition. The rainwater that damaged much of the sanctuary had no effect on the ark, built, as it was, into its own extension with its own roof. Because the ark remained un-opened during the synagogue's many years of decline, the lining also eluded oxidation.

On either side of the ark, built-in wooden benches provided seats of honor for the rabbi, distinguished visitors, and well-to-do members eager to pay for the privilege.

The eastern wall is completed by a pair of side arks, one in each corner. These contained the *haftorah* scrolls, the selections from the Books of Prophets which are read every Sabbath immediately after the reading of the Torah portion of the week.

The velvet-lined interior of the ark. Photo: © Kate Milford

Previous page: The Ten Commandment tablets above the ark were restored by EverGreene Painting Studios in time for the 2009 High Holidays after one of the tablets, misplaced for decades, was discovered as the Museum's collection was cataloged. Photo: Steven J. Selenfriend

Side ark. Photo: © Kate Milford

The most desired—and most expensive—seats were at the front of the sanctuary and faced the congregation. Photo: Edward Cheng

Directly in front of the ark is the
amud, an elaborately carved
walnut lectern and cantor's platform
with a balustrade and steps on
each side. In the early days of
American synagogues, cantors
were the liturgical equivalents of
opera stars: they were courted,
lured, pampered, and celebrated for
their vocal prowess and drawing
power. In fact, the synagogue's first
cantor, Pinhas Minkowsky, actually
contributed to the cantorial craze.
Already a sensation in Eastern
Europe, Minkowsky was considering
offers from well-established
congregations in Odessa and Vilna
when the Eldridge Street Synagogue
cablegrammed him a very appealing
offer. His signing with the synagogue
created an enormous stir, both
here and in Europe. This beautiful
amud attests to his importance
and befits the most temperamental
of tenors.

Whitney Cox

An elaborately carved Star of David (opposite) adorns the cantor's platform, which is attached to the front of the walnut *amud,* or lectern (above). Photo: © Kate Milford

The *bimah*, as seen from the women's balcony above. Photo: Whitney Cox

The *bimah*, the platform from which the Torah is read, is in the center of the sanctuary. Its placement there references the sacrificial altar in King Solomon's Temple and handily meets the Talmudic requirement that the chanting of the Torah be heard, and clearly, by all. Its location made the best use of the sanctuary's natural acoustics in an unamplified world. Like the *amud*, the *bimah* is surrounded by a carved wood balustrade and can be reached by two steps on either side. Brass torchieres adorn the four corners. The sanctuary fairly glows with the warm light of several beautiful brass light fixtures, most notably, the grand Victorian chandelier, which is suspended from the central dome. Originally lit by gas, its numerous arms and green-rimmed glass flowers were eventually turned downward to accommodate light bulbs. The chandelier is gracefully comple-mented by the *menorah*, which rises from the *amud*, and by the many lights in brass sconces attached to the walls and columns.

Basket sconces with a crown motif and topped with a Star of David flank the ark. Identical fixtures line the side aisles on both the main and balcony levels. Photo: Courtesy of Aurora Lampworks, Inc.

The crystal and glass "ladies' chandelier," originally a gas fixture, likely adorned the parlor of a congregant's home before being donated to add light and sparkle to the women's balcony. Photo: © Kate Milford

The main chandelier holds 75 individual lights. Photo: Laszlo Regos

Painted decorative patterns and finishes cover every surface of the sanctuary—walls, columns, capitals, coffers, wainscoting—employing almost every technique from pounce and stencil to *faux bois* in addition to *trompe l'oeil.* In a continuing effort to impress and aggrandize, inexpensive woods are made to look costly, lath and plaster are transmuted into marble, coffers and pendentives become three-dimensional.

Paint analysis uncovered two decorative paint schemes for the marbleized walls and columns. The first scheme was applied in 1894, when the sanctuary was lit by gas. The walls and columns were painted to look like stone in tones ranging from coral to taupe, with blue, gray, and white veining. The second scheme was applied in 1918, when lighter taupe, more consonant with the electric lighting, was introduced. It has been retained.

The second commandment forbids the making and use of any images, figurative or anthropomorphic, that might be perceived as the likeness of G-d, so all the patterns in the sanctuary are geometric or abstract or organic, like the seashells in the *trompe l'oeil* windows and the intertwining leaves and spade-shaped patterns, suggestive of Moorish styles, used throughout.

Other painted motifs include a blue firmament with gold stars and, of course, the Star of David.

Trompe l'oeil murals beside the ark depict *faux* wood panels, marble columns, seashell niches, and cloth covered windows. Photo: Whitney Cox

A hand-painted Star of David design decorates the ceiling in the synagogue lobby. Photo: Whitney Cox

The lobby walls are painted with a *faux* marble finish. The open doors to the left lead to the main sanctuary; the stairs at the back lead to the women's balcony. Photo: Whitney Cox

Like the walls, the woodwork has a polychromatic color scheme, as exemplified by the sanctuary pews. Their oak bodies, with trefoil cutouts, are lightly stained, and the mahogany caps of the end supports and the prayer book rests are darkly stained. The wainscot is grained with the oak color, and the chair rail has the deeper mahogany color. The floors are unadorned pine. Their worn grooves were made by the tread of thousands of worshippers moving their feet in praying patterns.

From this vantage point, standing on a humble pine floor, looking upward and around at such grandeur, who would not be inspired to dream big dreams?

And then, of course, there is the
natural light which vivifies the
sanctuary's magnificent collection
of original stained-glass windows.
There are 67 of them, in all, com-
prising more than 250 individual
panels, with over 600 small
"jewels"—windows of varying size,
design, and coloration; windows at
every level and on every wall, not
to mention in the stair towers and
foyer; windows in the shape of
keyholes and tablets and circles
that interlock or adjoin or stand
alone, each with a Star of David;
skylights, portals, oculi, a rose
window at each end—truly a
dazzling display of color and light,
of craftsmanship and preservation.
Because the building is freestand-
ing, abundant sunshine pours
in from all angles, suffusing the
sanctuary with the full spectrum
of gemstone hues.

   Many of the windows are
grouped in fives, suggesting
the Five Books of Moses.

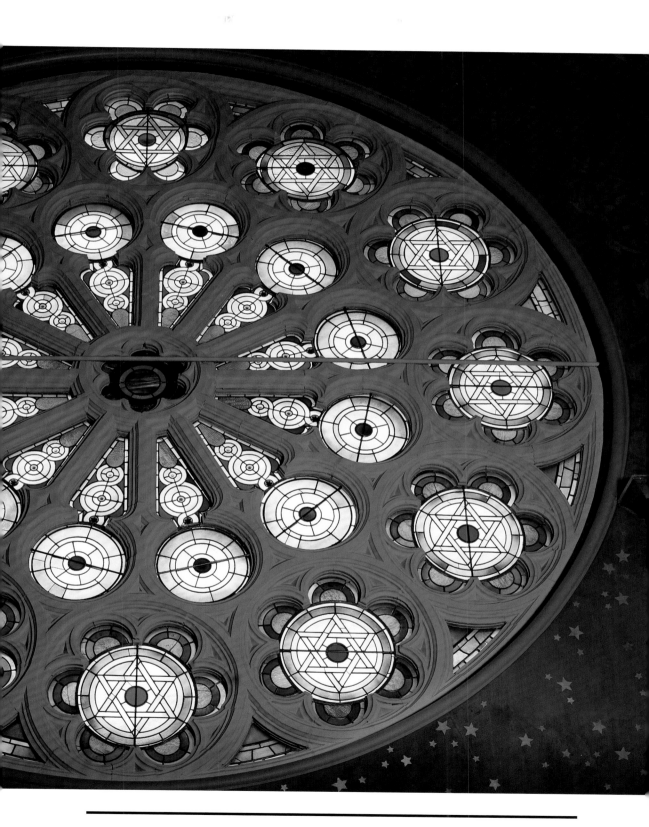

The rose window on the synagogue's western wall, as seen from inside the sanctuary. Photo: Whitney Cox

Five stained-glass windows, all with an identical pattern, line each side of the sanctuary. Artisans achieved remarkable variety and harmony by varying the colors used in each window. Photo: Whitney Cox

Above the entrance door leading from the lobby into the main sanctuary is a large stained-glass roundel with a crimson Star of David at the center. Photo: © Kate Milford

Light pours through the keyhole window at the top of the stairs to the women's balcony. Photo: © Kate Milford

Each side of the women's balcony is lined with five stained-glass windows, identical in pattern, but different in effect due to varied color schemes used by the original craftsmen. Photo: © Kate Milford

Clerestory windows with a "pie" design bring light to the sanctuary below. Photo: © Peter Aaron/Esto

Each side bay of the women's balcony features an arched stained-glass window and a small, richly decorated dome. Photo: © Peter Aaron/Esto

FACADE

The spectacular Moorish design of the synagogue's façade was a declaration of pride and arrival for the Jewish immigrant community of the Lower East Side.

INFRASTR

In 1938, a hurricane severely damaged the already compromised rose window above the ark. The congregation removed the window and boarded it up, hoping to replace it with stained glass in better times. By 1944, those times had not yet arrived, so plain glass blocks were installed in the shape of tablets at the doable cost of $750.

The blocks remained, in stark contrast to their surroundings, for more than 60 years, even after the main sanctuary reopened in 2007. As the restoration neared completion, one final question loomed—what should be done, if anything, with the east rose window? Unwavering in its commitment to historical authenticity, the Museum's Board was faced with a quandary. Should the glass blocks be left alone as a poignant reminder of the synagogue's decline, or should the original rose window be recreated? But no record of the original design existed. What then? A duplication of the west rose window? A new design in the old style?

Or perhaps a bold, new window, completely contemporary in its design and execution, one that would represent the newest chapter in the synagogue's story and demarcate the next phase of its history. No doubt, the founders of the Eldridge Street Synagogue had hoped that their synagogue would be a vital, living home for many, many generations. What could better signify the realization of their hopes than a twenty-first-century tribute to their nineteenth-century dream?

With great daring, the Museum's Board opted for modernity.

In 2008, the Museum solicited window concepts and designs from 12 glass artists of diverse backgrounds, some of international stature, others who were emerging. Each was asked to submit a design that would integrate with the sanctuary's existing aesthetic, architectural, and historic vocabulary. In 2009, renowned artist Kiki Smith and architect Deborah Gans were awarded the commission for their brilliant schema.

Their design followed a course of inspired simplicity. Not wishing to add any new visual elements to a high-Victorian interior already rich in visual elements, they extended into stained glass the existing

Previous page: Keyhole windows illuminate the rear of the women's balcony where an exhibit in the Wilks Family Gallery documents the synagogue's restoration. Photo: © Peter Aaron/Esto

For a dwindling congregation, glass blocks were an affordable replacement for the synagogue's damaged east rose window. Photo: Frederick Charles

firmament with five-pointed yellow stars
that is painted on the wall surrounding
the window, on the west wall, in the
ceiling domes, and in the *trompe l'oeil*
windows on either side of the ark. This
decorative motif was immensely popular
throughout America in the 1880s, when
the synagogue was built. Kiki Smith
speculates that "as people coming
from East Europe, retaining their own
identity as Jewish immigrants, they
used the Star of David on all the
windows. But then they used the
five-pointed star to say 'We are new
people here and we are part of the
fabric of the United States.'"

Only one other motif is used—the
six-pointed Star of David, from which
the ribs of the window radiate.

Through the use of modern flash-
glass and silicone technologies, the
new east window is a *trompe l'oeil* of its
own, one which intimates the fourth
dimension. Rendering the existing
motifs in this new way intensifies the
floating quality of the sanctuary's
surface and space and achieves an
aesthetic, emotional, and sensorial
unity with them. In a seamless sweep of
flight, the viewer moves from the interior
space to the space of the window, from
the past to the present to the infinite.

The new east window, designed by Kiki Smith and Deborah Gans, was installed in the fall of 2010.
Photo: © Peter Aaron/Esto

ABOUT THE STORATION

Courtesy of EverGreene Architectural Arts, Inc.

rom the incorporation of the Eldridge Street Project in 1986 through the grand re-opening of the main sanctuary in 2007, efforts to restore the Eldridge Street Synagogue were guided, with constancy of purpose, by two fundamental principles: historic authenticity and ecological sustainability. In the words of Roberta Brandes Gratz, "It is important to remember that what *was* here *is* here." And what *is* here is not only a model of architectural preservation, but a standard for the use of green technologies and practices in historic buildings.

With the restoration work spanning a 25-year period, the scope and the expertise needed to guide the work changed dramatically, focusing first on the development of the original structural report by Giorgio Cavaglieri. With time, the restoration strategy changed and a new plan was prepared by Jill Gotthelf with the firm of Robert Meadows Associates. Robert Silman came on as structural engineer and Martin Goldman and Reynaldo Prego as mechanical engineers. As Owner's Representative, Diane Kaese worked with architects, engineers and the construction manager throughout the work. Tim Allanbrook of Wiss, Janney, Elstner Associates was engaged as part of the team. Walter Sedovic Architects, who had since been joined by Ms. Gotthelf, developed the green conservation strategy and completed the interior restoration and exterior work. In a final flourish, the new east window was executed by a team led by artist Kiki Smith and architect Deborah Gans. Throughout most of the implementation, Terry Higgins, the construction manager, coordinated a team representing nearly 50 different stained-glass

A column receives a gilded capital and *faux* marble finish. Photo: Diane Kaese

artisans, architects, paint preservationists, lighting specialists, and contractors. The underlying strategy throughout was to salvage and conserve as much of the building's original fabric and materials as possible, without stripping away the synagogue's soul-stirring patina of time and experience.

As a result, nearly 85% of the glass, more than 95% of the wood, much of the original paint and plaster, and almost all of the brass fixtures are historic, and none of it is shined or enhanced or glossed to look like opening day 1887, or worse, to look like what never existed at all. What could not be salvaged and conserved was recycled, sometimes within the building itself. The wood used in the restoration of the south stairs, for example, came from the north stairs, which had completely collapsed from water damage.

Almost all the new materials added to the building are natural, eco-friendly, recycled and/or salvaged as well, from the lime mortar used to re-point the façade to the additional timbers for the stairs to the fly ash concrete in the southern stairwell and elevator shaft to the slate roof to the recycled plastic milk containers of the dividers in the cellar bathrooms and the recycled

blue jeans that now provide the building's insulation.

So as not to compromise the historical integrity of the main sanctuary, modernity, in the form of the large mechanical systems that heat, ventilate, and cool the building, was consigned to the cellar, along with the new bathrooms. Before 2004, however, there was no cellar. The creation of this 5000 square-foot level was one of the trickiest feats of the project and cost $2.5 million.

To protect the fragile structure, workers used hand shovels to dig up to 20 feet below the preexisting basement area, proceeding in four-foot sections, one section at a time in order to maintain the building's stability. Rock and river sand were removed by hand and conveyor belt. Similarly, underpinning was achieved by removing the soil in four-foot sections along the perimeter wall and replacing it with concrete. An exposed beam demarcates the old building material from the new, and an original pier remains to reveal the original structure and new underpinning.

The state-of-the-art mechanical systems include two energy-efficient boilers and programmable day-and-time thermostats that regulate the temperature, zone by zone.

A crawl space beneath the building was carefully excavated to create a new basement level for storage, an office, mechanical rooms, and public restrooms. Photos: Diane Kaese

Within a shallow crawlspace, brick piers supported the building. When a new cellar was excavated, deepening this space to hold an office, storage, and mechanical rooms, one of the original piers was left intact and visible. Photo: Jessica Schein

State-of-the-art mechanical systems were installed in the newly excavated basement. Photo: © Peter Aaron/Esto

The exterior of the building posed other challenges and inspired different choices. Lime mortar, rather than Portland cement, was used to re-point the façade because of its green qualities. An ancient material, lime mortar is natural, more flexible and durable than cement, more porous yet requiring far less water in its preparation, and simply beautiful to look at. According to construction manager Terry Higgins, its inherent flexibility allows "the whole building to act as a unified system." It also required the workers of the Seaboard Weatherproofing and Restoration Company of Port Chester, NY, to be trained in its usage. Apparently, it was love at first application.

So taken were they with the spirit of green, the Seaboard team willingly salvaged some bluestone pavers that were going to be discarded by a Jersey City construction company. The stones were used to re-pave some of the Eldridge Street areaways. In addition to re-pointing the masonry, Seaboard repaired the window surrounds, cleaned the brick, and restored the terra cotta around the center windows.

Exterior restoration required top-to-bottom scaffolding on both the back (opposite) and front of the building. Photos: Diane Kaese

A more complicated matter was restoring, or more accurately, recreating the seven original rooftop finials. As they weathered and disintegrated, they were deemed a hazard by the City's Department of Buildings and removed. Over time, their masonry bases had been reduced to rubble.

Although the finials were long gone by the time the restoration project began, an early watercolor of their design still existed and matched exactly the design of the finials on the sanctuary ark. With this corroborating evidence, the watercolor served as the blueprint for the new finials, now composed of stainless-steel frames, decorative fiberglass shells, and aluminum Stars of David fabricated by Gratz Industries. The bases were also recreated, and the finials were then hoisted into place by a 100-foot boom. In the spring of 2006, a ceremony celebrating the replacement of the central finial also marked the completion of the façade's restoration.

Leo Sorel

Mario Morgado

Hoisting the last finial into place on the synagogue roof in March 2006. Photo: Leo Sorel

Slate was used for the roof, not simply because it had been used originally, but because of its many sensible properties and its green superiority to asphalt. Slate is long-lasting, cost-effective over time, and fireproof. In addition, it reduces heat retention. Asphalt, on the other hand, is short-lived and flammable. Because it is an oil-based product, it also emits gasses when heated. Ironically, the building's original slate roof was damaged when asphalt shingles were nailed to it.

A worker balances at the building's front peak during the restoration of the slate roof and flashings.
Photo: Diane Kaese

The restoration of the painted finishes in the main sanctuary began like an archaeological dig and proved to be as layered and labor-intensive a process as the original application of the stencils and paints themselves. The work was conducted by EverGreene Painting Studios of Manhattan, which oversaw the paint restoration of the Chrysler Building, the Empire State Building, and the Metropolitan Museum of Art.

Initial paint analysis revealed the cambium rings of the synagogue's several paint campaigns. On the surface were grime and decay and washes of solid blue, pink, and tan that were applied in the 1940s, when the congregation could no longer afford to maintain the innumerable flourishes and details. A few careful scrapes of a scalpel unearthed the 1918 scheme, which better complemented the only recently electrified sanctuary. Beneath the 1918 scheme lay the darker 1894 scheme, and beneath that, the original scheme from 1887.

The 1918 scheme was chosen as the final destination. Reaching it would require the least amount of erasure and removal, and its lighter coloration was best suited for electric lighting. Mock-ups were done to determine which areas could be cleaned and conserved, which upper layers had to be removed and in-painted, which patches of delaminating paint could be re-adhered, and which sections were missing completely and had to be recreated.

Fortunately, the fabric was still intact on the ceiling and in most of the upper sections of the sanctuary. All they needed was a careful cleaning, but not so careful as to lose their patina of history. Elsewhere, if the original plaster was unstable, a sort of architectural Botox composed of chemical consolidants and adhesives was injected to create new plaster keys. Mechanical consolidations were effected with screws, washers, pins and tie wares. Finally, where there was significant water damage by the towers and along the exterior walls, new plaster was put in and the finishes were recreated.

Because the decorative details of the main sanctuary were stenciled and painted exclusively by hand, the EverGreene restorers used many of the same techniques and tools employed by the original artisans.

As is so often the case with the Eldridge Street Synagogue, the past and the present converge.

A "paint window" shows the 1918 decorative paint scheme beneath a more recent coat of blue.
Photo: Dan Weeks

Previous pages: From a temporary wooden platform built high above the sanctuary floor, artisans were able to work on the uppermost reaches of the walls and ceiling. They removed loose plaster to expose original lath in arches and domes before rebuilding, replastering, and restoring original paint finishes.

Injecting consolidants to save the original paint. Photo: Kumi Hisano

PANEL OF LATH, PLASTER AND BRICK

When the Eldridge Street Synagogue renovation first began, the main sanctuary was severely damaged. Temperature fluctuations and water infiltration had caused the plaster and paint to deteriorate. This panel reveals the several layers of the wall construction—brick, lath, plaster and paint. It also provides a window onto the renovation process. Note the bits of horsehair used to bind the plaster.

A section of exposed lath, plaster, and brick was retained to recall the building's former state of deterioration and to allow visitors to glimpse the interior structure of the walls. Photo: Peter G. Borg, Rider University

The paint team encountered many touchingly human mistakes their predecessors had made on their ambitious folk-art canvas—stencils which are off-mark, inconsistencies in the sizes and shapes of the patterned details, even the delightfully unexpected appearance of a single heart in one of the balcony pendentives, quite possibly a private message of love. In every instance, these mistakes have been retained. More than this, they are cherished.

Here and there in the main sanctuary, visual evidence of the proud and not-so-proud past has been intentionally retained as well, in tribute to the synagogue's life and history. A strip of the original 1894 paint scheme remains in one of the domes of the women's balcony and an exposed patch on the painted mural by the ark further provide a snapshot of the differences between paint schemes. A small, unrestored swath of wall in the northern section of the women's gallery chronicles the synagogue's sad decline and allows the viewer to peer through lath and plaster and horsehair binding, through time and space, into the body and soul of the building.

Light streams through the central oculus as scaffolding is erected at the start of the interior restoration.
Photo: Frank Hallam Day

Artisans restored the rose window on the synagogue façade and the painted decorations covering the interior walls. Photo: Whitney Cox

Working on a temporary wooden platform high above the sanctuary floor, artisans from EverGreene Studios uncovered the 1918 paint scheme, which featured a *trompe l'oeil* coffered vault and scroll designs.

Photo: Dan Weeks

The quest for authenticity extended to the restoration and conservation of the lighting fixtures and the grand Victorian chandelier in the main sanctuary. Time and water damage had once again taken their toll. Even worse, except for the chandelier, all the fixtures were lit by natural gas, the by-products of which are especially harsh on brass and glass. As a result, many of the hundreds of component parts had chipped, cracked, or corroded. Some had almost completely disintegrated.

It would have been far easier for Aurora Lampworks of Brooklyn, New York, to make new pieces rather than to repair the damaged ones, but an imperfect original was consistently regarded as superior to a perfect replacement. What resulted was a challenging, labor-intensive process whereby the corrosion was removed without further damaging the fixture and the original parts were repaired, complete with flaws.

The dozens of pieces that comprise the main chandelier were individually cleaned and polished before being reassembled. Photo: Courtesy of Aurora Lampworks, Inc.

Nearly all of the original crown-and-basket fixtures had disappeared over time. In fact, only one remained. Despite numerous consultations and collaborations, it was impossible to recreate its delicate piercings and embossed patterns using modern-day techniques. Dawn Ladd, owner of Aurora Lampworks, located a prominent expert in the field of chasing and *repoussé* who taught her the old-school way: heated pitch is poured into a metal "spinning" of the form and then the metal is chased, or cut into, by specially designed chisels.

The Eternal Light had to be recreated, as well, but unfortunately, there was no original to copy. Only a few old photographs contained its image. The form and proportions were carefully approximated, and a new griffin head was carved in clay and then cast in bronze. In another act of judicious recycling, the basket from the only remaining original crown-and-basket fixture found its way into the Eternal Light.

In an effort to replace the many missing glass shades that adorn almost all of the lighting fixtures, Aurora Lampworks located the original manufacturer in France. Although the century-old molds for the shades were found, sadly the delicate lacework of the originals could not be replicated.

A word about the bulbs—they are tungsten, and admittedly, less efficient than the fluorescent ones in the cellar and *bes medrash*, but obviously more authentic. This trade-off of green principles for historic authenticity is compensated for by a dimming system which not only recreates the ambient lighting of the 19th century, but which cuts down on electric consumption.

A craftsman puts the finishing touches on a crown light fixture before it is mounted around a column in the sanctuary. Photo: Courtesy of Aurora Lampworks, Inc.

Crown-and-basket light fixtures, featuring original etched green glass shades, top tall posts at the corners of the platform leading up to the *bimah*. Photo: © Kate Milford

A crown fixture encircles a column in the women's balcony. Because the many broken original etched-glass shades could not be reproduced, simple modern copies were used in their place. Photo: © Kate Milford

As for the woodwork, through a process called "freshening," the original shellac finish of the pews was ever-so-slightly warmed and spread across the wood, thus retaining the age, integrity, and gloss of the benches while minimizing the use of synthetic chemical finishes. Any additional retouching employed natural shellac derived from the lac insect. The ruts and grooves in the floors remain, memorializing the tread of the congregants in prayer. The floors were hand-sanded with steel wool and refinished the way they were.

Balcony woodwork was cleaned and *faux* finishes were restored. Photo: Diane Kaese

When the historic staircase leading to the women's balcony was completely rebuilt and reinforced, the original woodwork was tagged, removed, and set back in place. Photo: © Kate Milford

The stenciled pattern on the walls of the historic staircase leading to the women's balcony was recreated during the restoration. Photo: © Kate Milford

On "Clean and Shine" days, the public joined the restoration effort, cleaning the synagogue's woodwork.
Photo: © Kate Milford

Floor indentations, made as generations of congregants shuffled during prayer, were carefully retained.

Photo: Steven J. Selenfriend

Marble memorial plaques were cleaned and restored. Photo: Edward Cheng

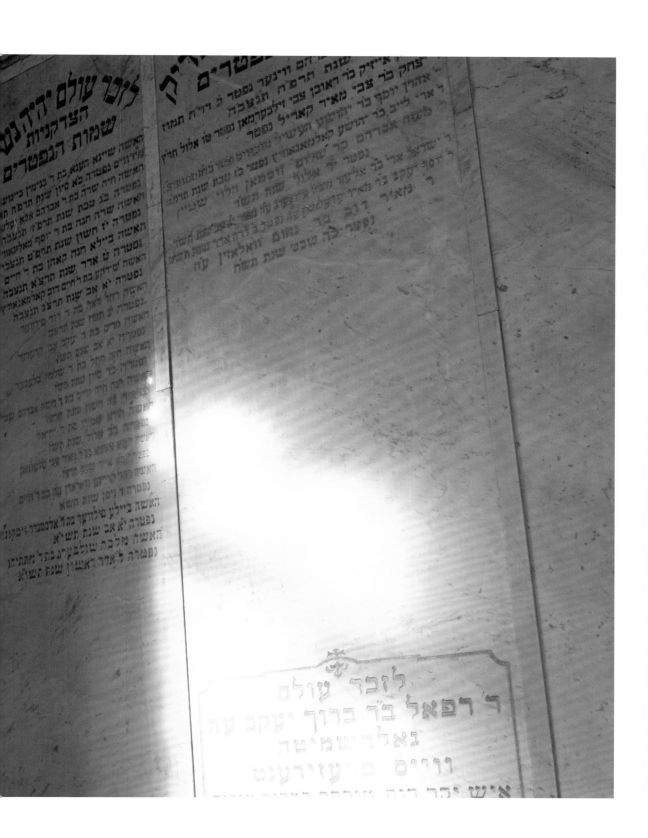

The restoration of the original
stained-glass windows by The
Gil Studio of Brooklyn, New York,
was painstaking. The location of
each stained-glass window differs
from that of the others because
of the forming techniques used in
the terra cotta or in the surrounds
for the windows. Again, the human
element prevails. A rubbing of each
window was done with crayon on a
piece of paper. All of the windows
were then carefully disassembled,
the existing glass was cleaned
and rinsed, the missing glass was
replaced, and the old, brittle lead
was removed. The glass pieces
were then placed into the outlines
of the rubbing, re-leaded and
refitted, pane by pane, window by
window. The recreation of the
many missing cast jewels was
particularly exacting—they came
in at least different ten styles, each
requiring four or five different colors.

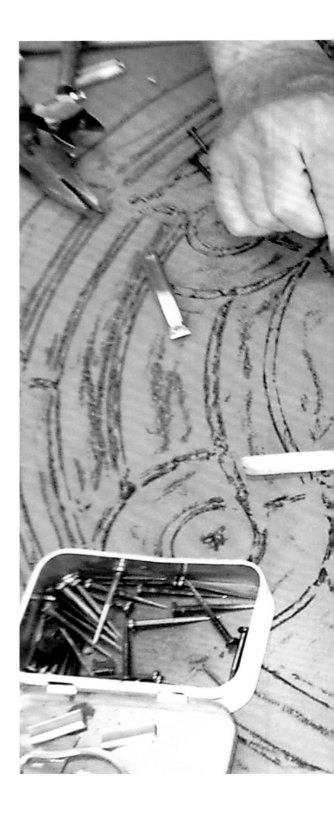

Individual stained-glass pieces were reassembled on rubbings made of each window's original leading.

Photo: Courtesy of The Gil Studio, Inc.

Top: Stained-glass panels were removed, brought to The Gil Studio and restored, then returned for reinstallation.
Bottom: Stained-glass jewels were recreated to replace lost features of the original windows.
Photos: Courtesy of The Gil Studio, Inc.

Restored panels of the west rose window were set back into place. Photo: Courtesy of The Gil Studio, Inc.

The sanctuary's only departure from historical accuracy is, of course, the east window. The creation of this window once again unites the old with the new in the Eldridge Street Synagogue, as ancient stained-glass techniques are teamed with modern silicone technology to produce an exciting contemporary work of art. Panes of Lamberts antique flash glass, a two-layered composite of clear and cobalt-blue glass, were cut into over 1,200 individually shaped pieces by artisans of The Gil Studio. And more than 650 stars were acid-etched onto the surface. The cobalt-blue sides of the glass were treated with silver stain to create the window's rich palette of blues, aquas, and yellows. The many pieces were then carefully placed, layer by layer, into silicone, atop a clear-glass substrate.

With this new technology, gone is the need for the leaded outlines of traditional stained glass windows. As architect Deborah Gans explains, "What would have been lines of lead are now lines of light." Gone, too, are the size restrictions for the glass panels. Thus freed from old limitations, artist Kiki Smith achieves a painterly fluidity, dimensionality, and intensity through the shading and layering of color. The central Star of David was cast in glass by artist Linda Ross.

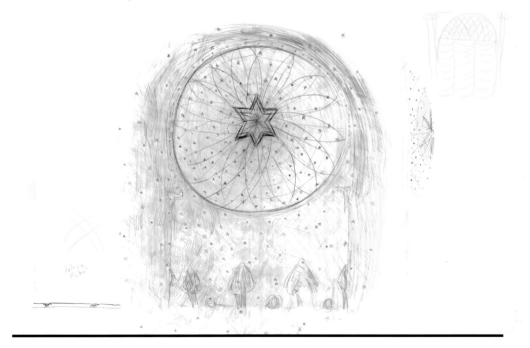

The initial concept for the new window. © Kiki Smith/Deborah Gans, 2009

Six large panels of layered glass, acid-etched with fields of stars, surround a central cast-glass Star of David. Photo: © Peter Aaron/Esto

A full-size paper cartoon guided the placement of the stars on the window. Photo: © Kiki Smith, 2009

At the center of the window, a thick metal frame will hold the cast-glass Star of David.

Photo: Timothy Allenbrook

The most technologically challenging part of
the window design was the frame, according
to architect Tim Allenbrook. "The spiral arms
and center star create a unique configuration
where each radial arm is subjected to a
twisting force when the wind blows against
the window. Since this must be compensated
for through brute strength, the frame
elements are fabricated from solid steel bars
as opposed to hollow metal tubes or, traditionally, wood. Because solid steel is not
a good insulator, an exterior, thermally
isolated protective glazing system has been
designed to minimize condensation, improve
energy efficiency, and protect the art glass
from damage."

Designed and created by Patrick Baldoni
and Art Femenella of Femenella & Associates
in Brooklyn, the frame is 16 feet in diameter
and weighs 4,400 pounds. It was hoisted into
place by a crane perched in the narrow lot
behind the synagogue. The six pie-shaped
stained-glass panels were then trucked to
the Lower East Side from Brooklyn, carefully
raised up to the "dance floor," a temporary
wooden platform erected inside the synagogue, and lifted into place by a team from
Femenella Designs. Finally, a protective
glass sheath was placed on the exterior
of the window. The entire process was
overseen by Eldridge Street's indefatigable
construction manager, Terry Higgins.

The steel frame for the new window is hoisted into place. Photo: Arthur J. Femenella

A team of workers from Femenella & Associates carefully lifts a section of stained glass into the window frame. Photo: © Kate Milford

As for the glass blocks that were
replaced by the new east window, they
remain a treasured feature of the
building. In keeping with the philosophy
of preservation that guided the entire
restoration, they are now set in a new
tablet-shaped frame which forms a
Tribute Wall in the Gural-Rabinowitz
Family History Center in the *bes
medrash*, forever a memory of difficult
times endured and overcome.

The installation of the east window
marks the official end of the quarter-
century restoration of the Eldridge
Street Synagogue.

In recognition of its magnificent
achievement, the Eldridge Street
Synagogue was honored with the
National Trust for Historic Preservation's
2008 Preservation Honor Award, the
Metropolitan Chapter of the Victorian
Society in America's Restoration Award,
the Municipal Art Society's Masterwork
Award for New York City's Best
Restoration Project, the New York
Landmarks Conservancy's Lucy G.
Moses Preservation Award, and the
Preservation League of New York's
Restoration Award. It was also listed in
The New Yorker's Architecture's Ten
Best of 2008 and *New York Magazine*'s
2008 Top Ten Designs.

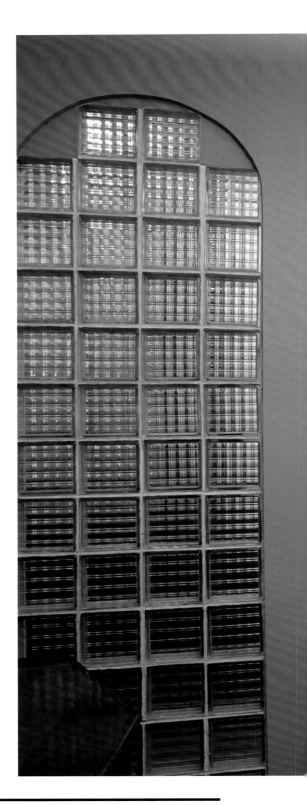

Previous page: Putting finishing touches on the new window. Photo: © Peter Aaron/Esto

Glass blocks removed from the east window were reassembled in a new tablet-shaped frame to form a Tribute Wall in the Gural-Rabinowitz Family History Center. Photo: © Kate Milford

IN THE

TWENTY FIRST CENTURY

rested from oblivion at the end of the 20th century, the Eldridge Street Synagogue enters the 21st century with pride and purpose and a debt to repay. What has been preserved, and magnificently so, is more than a grand old building with fanciful trimmings. What has been preserved is a way of life, a pocket of time, a chapter in the history of a country whose national character was forged by the spirit which built this building in 1887. The story of the Eldridge Street Synagogue is the story of America itself, and the Museum at Eldridge Street has as its mission the guardianship of that story and its retelling to this and future generations.

The Museum's timing is fortuitous. Today, the synagogue is a Jewish mirage in a Chinese landscape, a memory made permanent at the point of evaporation. Grandparents still bring their grandchildren to the synagogue to show them where they prayed, but they are becoming increasingly rare, even more the victims of time than the synagogue itself. When they are all gone, the Museum at Eldridge Street will still remain.

Edward Cheng

In the three short years since the
building was rededicated and the
doors re-opened, over 80,000 visitors
have come to the Eldridge Street
Synagogue—Jews and non-Jews
alike, from New York and beyond,
some with an emotional connection,
others with little more than curiosity—
tourists, teachers, and schoolchildren,
historians, lovers of art and architecture, devotees of lectures and concerts,
even couples wishing to be married
in the main sanctuary and parents
hoping to have their children *bar
mitzvahed* at the *bimah*.

   And so, the life cycle continues.

   The Museum at Eldridge Street
offers a bountiful bill of fare.
Comprehensive guided tours provide
thrilling proximity to the building's
many treasures as well as detailed
historical information about the
synagogue and its restoration.

Unni and Marc Chafiian take their wedding vows, August 2009. Photo: Craig Paulson

Max Smith, who was *bar mitzvahed* at the Eldridge Street Synagogue in 1927, and his wife Ruth attended the Museum's *Lower East Side Family Reunion* in December 2008. Photo: © Kate Milford

More than 50 original Eldridge Street Synagogue congregants and their descendants gathered for
a historic photo shoot at the *Lower East Side Family Reunion* in December 2008. Photo: © Kate Milford

In its continuing quest to engage and enrich
our children, The Museum at Eldridge Street
offers a variety of educational and family
programs. Each year, thousands of students
tour the Museum, sit in the synagogue's
pews, and travel back in time for a unique
view of our American past. Hundreds of
students of all faiths participate annually in
The Museum's *Celebrate With Us* program,
which commemorates the holidays of
Passover, Hanukkah, and Simchat Torah
with food, song, and festivities. The Museum's
Turn-of-the-Century Bar Mitzvah program
details the history and ceremony of this
essential Jewish rite of passage. During
the *Preservation Detectives* family program,
youngsters are given magnifying glasses,
binoculars, and notepads in pursuit of art,
architecture, and history.

In addition, hundreds of educators from
across the country come to New York each
year to participate in the Museum's professional development workshops. After an
intensive series of lectures, tours, and
discussion groups, the visiting instructors
develop lesson plans and materials on
the immigration experience for inclusion
in their school curriculums.

Mother and son enjoy the Museum's *Preservation Detectives* children's program. Photo: © Kate Milford

In addition to tours of the building itself, the Museum offers a variety of fascinating walking tours which highlight the neighborhood's rich history and culture, including the last vestiges of Jewish life in the modern-day Lower East Side; the many local sacred sites of the Jewish, African American, Hispanic, Italian, and Chinese immigration experience; the turn-of-the-century romantic hotspots, dance halls, and cafes; the lives of writer Sholem Aleichem, gangster Big Jack Zelig, and Rabbi Jacob Joseph, all of whom lived and died on the Lower East Side; and the area's boisterous political activity in the early twentieth century.

For those who are unable to visit the Museum, the Museum will visit you by way of its Traveling Landmark program, a beautifully illustrated slide-show presentation which serves communities nationwide.

In 2009, the Museum accessioned, cataloged, and photographed over 500 historical items that were long kept in storage. These comprise the Museum's permanent collection and include several generations of Torah mantles, ark curtains, *bimah* and Torah covers, wimpels, prayer shawls, tefillin bags as well as spittoons, Yiddish signs, a 1902 primer for Yiddish speakers learning English, and a variety of archival materials. Among the oldest artifacts is a gold silk-brocade ark curtain which predates the synagogue and references the congregation's former home on Allen Street. The 1882 curtain fits exactly the congregation's original Allen Street ark, which was carried to Eldridge Street in 1887 and is now housed in the street-level *bes medrash*.

The Museum preserves actual memories as well as art and artifacts. Its oral history collection contains a growing number of taped and transcribed interviews with former congregants, long-time residents of the Lower East Side, and the principals in the campaign to save the synagogue in the 1970s and 80s. A recent National Endowment for the Humanities grant enabled the creation of a state-of-the-art interactive learning center with large-format LCD displays. Taking its name from the Yiddish word for learning, the pair of *Limud* Tables employ modern technology to bring history and tradition to vivid life. One table details synagogue design and Jewish rituals and practices; the other uses a map of the Lower East Side as the digital starting point to the lost world of nineteenth- and twentieth-century Jewish immigrant life. Participants are even invited to assemble a turn-of-the-century Yiddish newspaper.

In October 2007, more than 100 of the world's most influential klezmer musicians were assembled for *A Great Day on Eldridge Street*, an unprecedented ten-day series of concerts, lectures, and educational events throughout New York State. The series kicked off with a photo shoot on the steps of the Synagogue, inspired by the iconic 1958 photograph "A Great Day in Harlem." This unique gathering of international musicians was conceived and led by violinist Yale Strom. Participants, who traveled to the Lower East Side from across the United States and around the world, included Jewish music pioneers Theodore Bikel, Don Byron, Adrienne Cooper, David Krakauer, Frank London, Andy Statman, Alicia Svigals, and John Zorn.

Museum visitors learn about the Eldridge Street Synagogue, its history, community, and congregants using interactive, touch-sensitive tables. Photo: Courtesy of Potion Design

A Great Day on Eldridge Street. Photo: Leo Sorel

Theodore Bikel, accompanied by Yale Strom, gets ready to march through the streets of the Lower East Side as part of the celebrations for *A Great Day on Eldridge Street*. Photo: Rachel Rabhan

The Museum's ambitious calendar of public events includes lectures on all aspects of the immigration experience, film screenings and slide shows, genealogy workshops, instruction on storytelling and memoir writing, preservation symposiums, book chats, and live concerts of Jewish and Jewish-influenced music— cantorial, klezmer, jazz, Yiddish, even Jewish-Cuban-Caribbean! But the largest and most popular public event by far is the Museum's *Egg Rolls and Egg Creams Festival*, a joyous celebration of Jewish and Chinese cultures. Each year, thousands of people crowd narrow Eldridge Street to partake of live music, mahjongg, Mandarin and Yiddish lessons, scribal and folk art, and of course, kosher egg rolls and refreshing egg creams.

In 2009, First Lady Michelle Obama designated the docents and other volunteers of the Museum at Eldridge Street as *Preserve America Stewards* in recognition of their outstanding commitment, excellence, and hard work. Of the 21 organizations that have been so honored, the Museum at Eldridge Street is the only one based in New York City.

Qi Shu Fang's Peking Opera Association performs at the Egg Rolls and Egg Creams Festival in 2007.

Photo: © Kate Milford

May you live to be 120 is the Jewish blessing for longevity. Now well past that milestone, the Eldridge Street Synagogue has indeed been blessed. With *mazel,* it will still be around, even as the Chinese on the neighborhood signs gives way to a different alphabet and that alphabet to its successor as the story of America continues to unfold. Like the people for whom it was built, the Eldridge Street Synagogue stands in triumph and exclaims, *l'chaim!*

AFTERWORD | A LOVE STORY

BONNIE DIMUN, EXECUTIVE DIRECTOR
MUSEUM AT ELDRIDGE STREET

I was hired with the mandate..."GET IT DONE."

In 2007, I assumed the executive directorship of the Eldridge Street Project. Prior to my appointment, a team of architects, artisans, specialists, sponsors, the Board of Directors, and staff had worked for more than two decades on the restoration of the 1887 Eldridge Street Synagogue. During that period, they secured New York City and National Historic Landmark status for this magnificent building and raised millions of dollars for the complete restoration of the almost crumbling outside walls, the restoration of the slate roof and skylights, and the creation of a new basement level with new mechanical systems. What they shared was a project of love, fueled by all the dedication, commitment, and funding they could garner to complete the restoration of this historic landmark synagogue. But it was not yet completed.

So, with the leadership of the Board of Directors and the most incredible staff of professionals I had ever encountered, we set a date for completion. It was truly the most exciting nine months of my professional life. Twice before I had nine months to experience the miracle of birth; this qualified as my third time.

We agreed that December 2, 2007, would be the date to rededicate the glorious Eldridge Street Synagogue. With the date set, everyone was mobilized. The target provided a collective shot of adrenaline...and everyone saw the date as a realistic goal.

During those nine months, with a masterfully choreographed schedule, artisans worked nonstop to meticulously put the finishing touches on this labor of love. Bright brass light fixtures were reassembled and installed; paint finishes were artfully completed; century-old woodwork was cleaned and polished; reassembled stained-glass windows were hoisted back into place.

Three days prior to the rededication, there were still those who said we would never make the deadline. We were at the wire. Happily, we proved them wrong, and the great event took place. All those involved—the many descendants of the original congregants and those who financially supported this project—joined together to rejoice in this spectacular achievement.

With the restoration completed, one question remained: what, if anything, to do about the synagogue's east window? Our Board's daring move paid off. In 2010, a magnificent 21st-century work of art by Kiki Smith and Deborah Gans was added to our 19th-century interior. Present meeting past could not be more harmonious.

Along the way, we focused our attention on the enhancement of our successful cultural and educational programs. In 2008, in recognition of the quality of our public services, the State of New York and the New York State Board of Regents granted museum status to our organization, now renamed the Museum at Eldridge Street.

And in 2009, First Lady Michelle Obama recognized the Museum's volunteer docents for their exemplary service by presenting the Preserve America Stewards Award to Eldridge Street. And the best is yet to come.

This book is *Beyond the Façade*. It is the story of the years of love, commitment, and dedication of people who believed in the importance of saving this critically significant American-Jewish heritage site. It is the story of one generation's deep respect for the sacrifices and memories of earlier generations. It is also a story of preserving our history as a means of strengthening our identity.

I am grateful to be part of that legacy. I invite you to visit this beautiful site, to enjoy our cultural and educational programs, and to learn about our rich history.

BIBLIOGRAPHY

PUBLICATIONS

Polland, Annie. *Landmark of the Spirit: The Eldridge Street Synagogue.* New Haven and London: Yale University Press, 2009

Cole, Diane. "Joy on Eldridge Street." *Preservation* March/April 2008

Davidson, Justin. "Reconstructionist Judaism." *New York Magazine* January 7, 2008

Gagne, Nicole. "Saving a Synagogue." *Traditional Building* December 2006

Gray, Christopher. "Eldridge Street Synagogue: A Prayer-Filled Time Capsule from the 1880s." *New York Times* May 19, 1996

Rothstein, Edward. "Return of a Long-Dormant Island of Grace." *New York Times*, December 1, 2007

MUSEUM AT ELDRIDGE STREET ARCHIVES

Eldridge Street Synagogue Master Plan. Robert E. Meadows, P.C. Architects. New York, 1991

Museum at Eldridge Street Annual Reports, 2007-2009

Museum at Eldridge Street Restoration Timeline

Museum at Eldridge Street Press Release: "Museum at Eldridge Street Commissions Artist Kiki Smith and Architect Deborah Gans to Create New, Monumental East Window for 1887 Eldridge Street Synagogue," November 19, 2009

National Historic Landmark Nomination for the Eldridge Street Synagogue, United States Department of the Interior, National Park Service National Register of Historic Places Registration Form

WEBSITES

Museum at Eldridge Street, www.eldridgestreet.org

Aurora Lampworks, www.auroralampworks.com

Wikipedia entries, "History of the Jews in the United States" and "Eldridge Street Synagogue," www.wikipedia.org

**Contributing Photographers
and family donations of photographs**

Peter Aaron/Esto
Timothy Allenbrook
Aurora Lampworks, Inc.
Peter G. Borg, Rider University
Edward Cheng
Frederick Charles
Martha Cooper
Whitney Cox
Frank Hallam Day
Francis Dzikowski/Esto
EverGreene Architectural Arts, Inc.
Arthur J. Femenella
Deborah Gans
The Gil Studio, Inc.
Kumi Hisano
Idelson Family (Rabbi Idelson)
Frank Jarmuth Family
    (Sender Jarmulowsky)
Diane Kaese
Kate Milford
Mario Morgado
Ozier Muhammed
Craig Paulson
Potion Design
Rachel Rabhan
Laszlo Regos
Jessica Schein
Steven J. Selenfriend
Kiki Smith
Lee Snider
Amy R. Sperling
Leo Sorel
Dan Weeks
Yood Family (Rabbi Yudelovitch)

Museum at Eldridge Street
12 Eldridge Street
New York, NY 10002
www.eldridgestreet.org